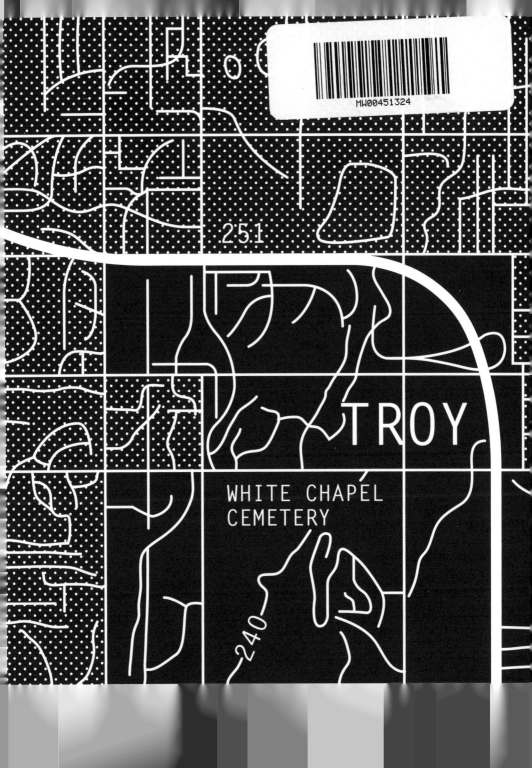

251

TROY

WHITE CHAPEL
CEMETERY

240

TROY, MICHIGAN

FUTUREPOEM BOOKS
NEW YORK CITY
2014

TROY, MICHIGAN

Wendy S. Walters

first edition | first printing

This edition first published in paperback by Futurepoem books
P.O. Box 7687 JAF Station, NY, NY 10116
www.futurepoem.com

Executive Editor: Dan Machlin
Managing Editor: Jennifer Tamayo
Copy Editor: Ted Dodson
Additional thanks to: Chris Martin, Francesca DeMusz
Guest Editors: Jen Hofer, Tisa Bryant, Simone Forti

Cover design: Everything Studio (www.everythingstudio.com)
Interior design: HR Hegnauer (www.hrhegnauer.com)
Typefaces: Letter Gothic (cover), Spectrum (Text)

Printed in the United States of America on acid-free paper

State of the Arts

NYSCA

This project is supported in part by the New York State Council on the Arts
with the support of Governor Andrew Cuomo and the New York State
Legislature, as well as by our Kickstarter backers, individual donors and
subscribers. Futurepoem books is the publishing program of Futurepoem,
Inc., a New York state-based 501(c)3 non-profit organization dedicated to
creating a greater public awareness and appreciation of innovative literature.

Distributed to the trade by Small Press Distribution, Berkeley, California
Toll-free number (U.S. only): 800.869.7553
Bay Area/International: 510.524.1668
orders@spdbooks.org
www.spdbooks.org

PROLOGUE, 1970s

Imagine you love sky enough to embrace
snow in right neighborhoods outside one
gray city. The tension between here and
there sets your expectation of distance.
This suburb wrangles a type. Maybe you
know them. Maybe you don't care who you tell.
That is the hope and question. To start, take
a shortcut through the woods. Feel the desire
for safety as you unfold the map. You
are almost home but not allowed to care
where it is. Try to find the clearing.
Houses along turning roads, each a false
fortress, don't fit together. Disquiet
serves as the provocation, the lesson.

ORIGIN MYTHS

The writer tumbles down the hill, her pen
dangerously sharp to her eyes. She does
not see old agonies shoot across skies
like the edge of Aurora, a hand-fan
of light waving, unfolding. The writer
ridicules sentiment, what she calls "bear,"
for resting in trees. I am one who got
away in heroic time with the help
of the small-town archivist. This saga
matters as much to me as epics do
to everyone else. Our chorus sparks their
ignitions, but engines don't turn over.
In the dark, the distance between mythic
and local is zero or omnibus.

DIGAMMA / STIGMA

A sound was lost between two leaning walls.
Outside a city of bronze shining dim
vanished into legend. You know that one—
Helen and her face, the men and their war,
the saga of empire, the sea. Our myths
disappeared, too: tales of hanging drywall,
planting gardens, watching soccer practice
at dusk. Instead of heroes, we became
bumps and potholes on the surface, slowing
the road. We craved expansion, new lots
cleared by diggers and backhoes. Anywhere
else gets an epic, why not us? Our lives
ringing true as bells without a clapper.
Go open the great gates to the city.

I L I O N

City on a hill, what ambitions you
cast centuries forward with your name.
Points manifest west, each a little less
auspicious than the last one called Troia.
Factory-fueled towns, fated to fall hard
from industry, towns that stole trees to claim
wealth and esteem as aspiration, then
turned soil to grit, will not die either.
You remain too far away from triumph
to claim a legacy, but still this trick,
naming a new city for a defeated
one, is to commit to optimism.
Fools navigate the end of an era
seeking direction in a starless sky.

OUT OF TROY, NEW YORK

Who knows which city was the first to Troy
if all states claim some version of the fall?
Upstate New York in Rensselaer County,
where Uncle Sam the butcher is buried,
is ancient America enough to start.
Textile kings in "Collar City," grand
launderers, invented an industry. Some
men were called to dirt instead, to dig and
seed to grow. Covered wagons roll Erie
Canal. Covered wagons roll Ohio.
Michigan shimmers in rivers and lakes
like nowhere at all. A Troy made again
invites myths of walled cities and idols
of speed into the woods to undo us.

MEMOIR

This is not a map. References betray
obvious injuries for fact. At the start, she
envisioned an "I" who overcame my
sensitivity to confession and
broke skin. No place reveals a single point,
time changes people. She became one more
version of herself. I witnessed the absence
of record and wrote it down in pencil.
Obtuse angles lengthen origin myths.
She called me up because I did not want
to vanish. Gone where I started from,
she invented this book of lists. She put
story fragments in order by color.
She let the woods entangle history.

HISTORY

Triumph over topography. The will
of prescient men. Fables of raising
class. Some likelihoods of industry.
The wheels of societal engineers.
Notable misfits of privilege grabbing
at status. Shadows over those for which
photographic evidence exists. Lore
not recounted in song. Understatement
for affect. Rumor disproven but turned
way up. Discarded ideals for small laws.
Arrogance as earnestness or malice.
The will of paying customers. Men who
die attempting to disprove the future.
Why gentle people get left out of this.

MAP

Through a fault in prescience, Ptolemy's
map of the world did not note the Midwest.
Vesconte knew the secret to a state's
well-being is how well its shore retains
mystery. Michigan, so far inland
it could be at sea, is reachable by
foreign ship if one knows how to follow
dying wind. Stereotypes and lithographs
invited the circumspect to migrate
here. Drawings, dark with detail, defined
perceptible depths. If printed, a map
turns public, loses its aura. Once we
go everywhere, no Jerusalem gets
torn down before the rise of another.

PLAN

Avoid mixing themes of development
with sentiment in efforts to accept
sprawl as abstract time. Population growth
creates a need to build infrastructure
as impulse clusters, one box at a time.
To make easy work of the territory,
name a state for water. Chart a river
through loam-rich farmland and grow a city.
Typify permanence as cul-de-sac.
Forget ardor for trees, forests, or fields.
Do this here or everywhere, fabricate
an American age free from conflict
not even a tinge of remorse. The air, dry
as paper, shows no signs of changing seasons.

FOUNDING

Start with some common interests in escape.
A dog treed a black bear and two cubs near
the edge of Alva Butler's land in 1829.
Samuel Williams roused twenty neighbors, who
rolled in two gallons of whiskey to make
more of their fear. Envision the ruckus
when mother and one cub break free. Men drank
through the night until Luther Webster quit
his friends to shoot down that final bear.
Less violent tales noted eminent men.
Reuben Beach, a childhood survivor
of shipwreck, bought acres in early Troy
though not as much ground as the distiller,
Johnson Niles, born in upper New York.

Johnson Niles, born in upper New York,
served as the town's first postmaster, justice
of the peace, county commissioner, and
leader of the Democratic Party.
Accused of selling alcohol to a
Nippising man by grand jury, he claimed
to have been made an honorary chief.
Because no law prevented one tribal
member from selling booze to another,
charges were dismissed. Niles and his wife,
Rhoda, instructed their sons George and Orange
in privilege but no wealth exceeded
the trees in their reach. After Rhoda died,
the housekeeper, Kate Steele, assumed her place.

The housekeeper, Kate Steele, assumed her place
in front of the camera when Mr. Niles'
requested. Her *carte de visite* invited
chatter that he admired her beyond
decency. In 1838, just after the bank
panic of 1837, Niles mapped out sixteen
blocks to form a village called Hastings,
so called for the president of the Bank
of Michigan. Because no railroad came
through here, only sixty folks called this place
home in the 1870s. A map of Oakland
County in 1857 suggests Troy's one
true road led to more significant towns.
Archives include personal depictions.

Archives include personal depictions.
"Daugarian Artist," J. Henry Russell,
who lived with his divorced mother, Charlotte,
served as the town's first photographer, though
he also worked as a tinsmith, hardware
merchant, and wood turner. Russell may
have taken the wedding photo of Charles
and Nell Aspinwall in 1880. The bride wore
a dark, embellished dress, her finest one,
although she did not survive pregnancy.
Death was not unusual for the time.
Among neighbors, class aspirations
rooted in clay like shrubs. Faith predicted
the advantage of larger families.

The advantage of larger families
was boundlessness, was why town markets
prospered. Samuel Levy's general
store in Big Beaver Village, next door to
a blacksmith, boasted the first telephone
in the area. Up the street children
gathered during recess to watch August
Schultz shoe horses and repair wagon wheels.
Beyond church, activities for women
included the Farmer's Club and Bay View
Reading Circle. Ladies shucked corn and picked
apples beside their husbands. By 1917, Ford
manufactured tractors to match the pace
of deer that fled from cultivated fields.

Of deer that fled from cultivated fields,
momentum left a trail of crushed clover
as new trucks hauled apples to a city.
For five decades they would endure the shock
of dirt and gravel roads. In these sweetheart
years, the children of factory workers
filled the one room Poppleton Schoolhouse.
Reciting the pledge taught kids how to curb
the impulse to fight. They learned how to draw
power through wires for electric light.
Raising a family during the war
sufficed as vigor. Anyone here might
have been kin until 1955 when planners drew
a map of a city over the town.

A map of a city over the town
makes it easy to forget where here is.
How can anyone discern who belongs
to this tradition of names and faces
blending in? Then down tumbles sugar-snow.
Picture a fat-armed work ethic. Detroit
assembly lines integrate first, foreshadow
discomfort. Some people worked hard to build
this place, color never factored in—
Nice for families: new roads freshly plowed,
every home deep in its yard, every yard
imitating one around the corner.
If you want to relate to your neighbors,
start with some common interests in escape.

OAKLAND COUNTY, MICHIGAN, 1877

Here, in the forest's wild seclusion,
no augury thwarts a promise of sky.
Long winters turn reticence into whim
when a shallow wind ignites ice. The fog
sizzles. Sylvan hills yield to roads and towns
built with an eye to homes left long ago.
A vista gets shaped by uninspired
impulse when cities plan rows and boxes.
The brightest moments of a blessed life still
spill over at the edges. The mind knows
a bloodless heart has no use. From the first
pastoral wanderings, a touch of somber
remembrance dims the blithesome green.
Visions of deeper solitude ripen.

KIN

Looks like one of us favors some of us.
What we know of us, no one else can know.
We invent the rules then decree the rules,
make them of us. We worry in the dirt.
We claim a town of ground. Once we should be
kin, relations blend in tight. This way we
win at church. Time to join the search on earth
for God in house. We trust our mouths to sing
of God in house, lightning in our kitchen.
Let us pray for food. We steal to better
share the good. We seek guidance in the woods.
To arrive right, we study light. We find
the best of us is us plus us and all
who promise they will stay this way for us.

DETROIT, 1967

Before the middle-class turned illusive
from faults of compromise, a gray city
inspired folks to think privilege is a
brick house: to live in it is to keep it.
We left off for work in a hurry, our
tools still hooked to the wall. With gratitude
we claimed, *Someone else invented this life.*
Myths of American genius are made
out of cities, too: civic mettle can
outlast the whims of industry. That's when
a city burns and history devolves
into fables of ruin and renewal.
Here comes nostalgia for days when the blade's
sharp edge provoked the courage to grab it.

DETROIT, AFTERMATH

A highway is a river for those who crave
bridges but will not cross a precipice
out of shame for loneliness. Some stalled
desires float on wind. At the thaw, ice
floes jam downriver. The sun gleams dim: it
cannot show itself. A new low-pressure
system means the industry plan for our
future includes seatbelts and latches, locks
and window cranks, all tools of containment.
What do we know of the end of the road
when here come the trash-men with their habit
of denting cans? The truck's monstrous chaw
cannot demolish every wish. Its lights
ignite the immovable agony.

HIGHWAY

Concrete below them, cars full of women
and men dressed in their regular costumes.
How curious the hundreds that ride seem
returning home, even if they are not
in each other's meditations longer
than a glance at the odometer. Storms
roll in from the west. This is how color
furnishes affection for distance then
foils their ability to withhold
distraction from eternity. Reach on
asphalt, reach beyond the roads' soft shoulders,
let the sublime roll out as vacant lots.
Prove the soul can find its natural home
pursuing romance with the horizon.

MICHIGAN

How many times did she mistake romance
for a continuum between weather
and myth? If she came back tonight, she could
not confuse the wind in her voice or crows
in trees for the end of optimism.
Every memory, some water. The moon,
fog-swaddled and razor-slim, exports its
cool to Sudbury and Baffin Island.
In order to claim the idea of North,
a Michigan moon skips the surface
of a lake six times before sinking. If
she follows it down, who can prove the lake
was not a sky? Her ambition leaves no
trace of the bluster that had been her name.

BLUEPRINT

With four exits on the interstate, Troy
at fast glance, appears to be twice its size.
One plan for the city, though not approved,
involved building a downtown of business
and housing units. A fear of mixed-use
space reflected mistrust, a solitude
philosophy. Families positioned
themselves against the coming world with stuff
made to break. Then they did, too. Anxiety
replaced any demands to be let in
or left out of the wasteland. A problem
with language is direction, the flatness,
though one should not avoid the cohesion
of a roadbed, if wanting to travel.

PLOT

The blueprint confirms planned indifference
for a landscape though it lacks key details,
like who looks out the window?
First, the surveyor counts the stones between
my ideal home and yours. Every lot squared
and stacked against each other clarifies
the look and tempo of development.
Broken or wavy lines over leveled ground
imitate elevations and contours.
Standard home designs model upstanding
neighborliness, how to wear a fair face.
People cannot predict other people.
A compass or directional arrow
indicates the plot's orientation.

HOUSE / YARD

A rhombus inside a rhombus offends
no one. Anyone could flee as bird/ horse
if impulse bests reason. Lay the map flat
and watch its folds settle. No fluttering
will right one's sense of direction. Figure
a child/ predator knows the balance
of little regret. Smoke from the chimney,
an elaborate image of warmth, shows
confusion between inside/ forest or
fire/ breeze. One leans on another or
one fails to commit when the other stays
true. Sometimes being surrounded comforts
loneliness. Sleep mirrors leveling
uneven terrain as the hours shook.

BUSINESS DISTRICT

Night patrol at the office park protects
emptiness. Curvilinear roads miss
imagined obstacles. Private access
converts bigots into quiet neighbors.
Someday they may let go of expectations,
a view of history from the fear side.
By feat of turnstile, the throng enters
the middle-class, pool at capacity.
A special look must be accomplished.
In echoing houses, there are no ties
but maybe a style of growing up.
Families crawl outland to landscaped lots
with barbed hedges. The pathway to the door
looks clear. Everything is temporary.

SPRAWL

This new math forbids simplicity
in the design of towns if nature
must be bulldozed before replanted in
a grid. A five-minute walk from center
to periphery frames a neighborhood.
Le Corbusier scratched blueprints on clouds
in 1929: *The street wears us*
out. It is altogether disgusting!
Why, then, does it still exist?
By 1969, traffic vanquished
all hope of bucolic serenity.
Solitude sells to those privileged to buy
suburban plots in the conspiracy
to claim concrete as proof of abundance.

RESIDENT

Imagine unwelcome with greater haste
than ambivalence. You are obtrusive
for reasons you can't understand, justly
dispensable, a symbol of fitting
agony, an instance of failed ideals
about liberty. Forget specifics
when you stand for tempo and metaphor
in the local debate on losing place.
Now go back to your seat in the corner,
anticipate lessons on shapelessness
as you testify to why you fit in.
A description of a typical you
confirms utopia will not happen
here if fear inspires lack of vision.

DRIVEWAY

The approach to the house imitates
one flat piece of rock. But you own this road.
It dead-ends at a yard as if stopping
by reflex answers the same intention
as building home. Fabrication invites
trespass while neighbors admire your lot
from over there. Enough distance allows
romances with other people's trouble.
Arguments fly from their houses. A string
tightens then breaks, one more lost kite. To stand
on this slab of slag and fly ash means you
have no perspective. The world might be what
you expected, benign as providence.
Wait here. Everything is coming to you.

WINTER

Under overcast skies, children practice
blame and violence better than gloominess.
Since all they know vanishes in the flash
of a blizzard, no one expects to be
found if lost in the woods behind the house.
Oak limbs drag, black with the dumb weight of ice,
then snow falls. It covers their feet like
bedclothes. Whiteness surrounds them like music,
downy to the ear. Through a dark window,
the street blurs, a moon's gravity ruined.
Porch lights left on all night will not reveal
why some kids lack empathy or how long
it will take them to shed their anger, feel
longing that leads them to gentler people.

WOODS

Leaves on tall boughs make the sound of applause
in the distance. When rain bends trees, here comes
longing. A girl studies the plot of these
woods for proof of her feelings—a tangled,
shadowy boscage, the creekbed's stalled mud.
The girl hides from those who don't seek her out.
An impulse to build in all directions
starts with seasons of birds or seeds aloft
then rooting in lawns or unkempt gardens.
Time to sabotage intruding saplings
if what they foment is thicket, more dusk.
From the damp mulch, a sky appears cracked
by new branches pulled too far from the root,
more untold aspirations falling down.

. . .

Hackberry. Hawthorn. Hickory. Blackgum.
Trembling Aspen. Beech. Maple. Musclewood.
Crabapple. Dogwood. Paw Paw. Oak. Oak. Oak.

NIMBUS

A sky scratched half-blue, a child's drawing.
The grass softens towards her. God is near
but not more free than she is. This brown hand
on your face is a girl who expects clouds.
Then she is me, looking dull as paper.
Now she rides her red bike one block over
to the reservoir. A world this small fades.
Even a bevy of hornets dissolve,
ellipses of emotion in pale light.
Down the street, a house on fire flickers
out. Now she longs to kiss a boy who smells
of smoke and hay. She will not get it yet—
why she needs to give in to impulse,
discard reason for the cool taste of clay.

FEAR

Look at them looking like they don't know
how they look. Why don't they just stay where they
stay? Or drag sideways across our fields, come
at us zigzag over the rows we cut.
We made a place they know they should not stay
for a reason. They were nothing back when
we started from nothing, or we could not
have worked so hard to be right. They never
do what they need to do to be right. Who
knows? Someone might kill one. We tell them this
if they don't run. *Come on, try us,* we say.
A city grows over the rows we cut.
Then they come at us. We stay for reasons.
They don't understand right the way we do.

OAKLAND COUNTY, MICHIGAN, 1976

Back then a fear of strangers did not feel
small-minded. Too many outsiders lived
in neighborhoods. Why not predict trouble
from mixing? A weakness in the bloodline
or faith forgotten turned winter icy
slick. Around the county, impossible
news provoked whispers—Mark Stebbins, age twelve,
vanished February 15. Four days
later, his body placed in a snowbank
as if sleeping. A slow, verdant season
of disbelief followed. Oblivion
reinstated the doldrums. But when Jill
Robinson, also twelve, vanished December
22, police took our fingerprints at school.

THE OAKLAND COUNTY
CHILD KILLER, 1977

Why recount details beyond facts of fate
when the lack of love shown remains unsolved?
Kristine Mihelich bought a magazine
from a convenience store on January 2.
On March 16, Timothy King's sister
loaned him thirty cents for drugstore candy.
Days after disappearing, their bodies
were left in the snow along a major
road like the children abducted last year.
The FBI launched its biggest manhunt
to date, but no indictments ever came.
Riding in cars, we studied the shoulders
of roads for small bodies like our own, proof
violence roots like ragweed, grows everywhere.

STOLEN

Any direction one looks at the sky,
someone falls away from the universe.
The air of colder seasons pushed through walls
and doors, promised to expose bone. This
is not the kind of loss one should romance,
but I did not understand what made them
so wanted. Envy made me lure sorrow
early on, court pain through acrobatic
feats of desire. I confused leaving with
abduction, family with calamity.
I could not recall a time before kids
went missing from sidewalks, so say I had
no perspective. I practiced vanishing
to find I had always been somewhere else.

CHARACTER

Because I was wrong to bring up the past,
the writer has drawn a version of me
that insists on being subject rather than
implement. Please think of her face instead
of your own if you want to empathize
with my error. Maybe you see her drift
through the atmosphere, trying to arrest
our pursuit of insight. She will not harm
your memories if you let the writer
mock your need to express awkward feelings.
The writer illustrates our girl's worries
as a wall of windows. Look out. See how
she waves as she walks up the road? She wants
you to join her, but you can't catch up.

LESSON

First the brown girl traced the outline of her
pink partner's body then her partner turned
her into shadow. Because metaphor
holds no nuance in kindergarten, what
else could they have chosen? Our girl *is* (a) black.
Her mother gasped when she saw the image,
a waxy minstrel with white eyes and red
mouth splayed as if floated up from the sea
in stalled anguish. What part of the lesson
taught them not to see? What task demanded
a page for this shapelessness? You should know
what the mother did fixed it: she redrew
her daughter brown. Then, because she had no
choice—crossed out the partner, teacher, and school.

CAFETERIA

Our girl forgot to bring lunch. Her mother
entered the lunchroom with brown paper bag,
heels hitting hard, legs kicking open her
white rabbit fur, turquoise dress fluttering
in rayon. Loose chignon, tortoise-shell shades
finished the cut. All affect aside, this
woman stunned the kids to whispers. Our girl
welled with admiration and gratitude.
The second grade class sang from the risers,
We tried to put what we see in language
you would understand. In 1978, the world
resembled no romance with possibility.
Everyone deserved a weapon. Mother
secreted her lighter, notebook, and knife.

RIGHT GIRLS

She is not them. They lure with scarcity.
Her profile suffers from scrutiny.
Though awkward, she attempts to blend in,
ignoring exclusion. Once she becomes
a "character," she loses introspection.
She is brown-skinned, yes, and her mother marched.
Estimate her drive to play tough, cruel
with fear. I give you two chances. I give
you a ball, a rope, a rhyme for your time.
The scars she showed, they don't quite see, so she
is done with present tense. The cost of your
reach will be incalculable, just like
pleasure. When she was a child, she did
not know her face would become everyone.

PICK ME

If her face could be one of the winners,
what hope exits a side door? Oh how
she longs to be taken but plays too shy
at awkward angles. Schoolyard blacktop show:
girls take out their ropes, choose teams by desire,
Who do they most want to be? Those of us
left out by ritual want our own sport,
some test of integrity. It will take
years to know for certain she is not quite
fit for these kicks. Some hammer stuck between
Why not? and *Maybe not?* You could call a foul,
but who would judge their disdain as cruel
when disregard good kids bandy about
hits those who do not matter anyhow?

UNSAID

Not quite rage, but a feeling just as sharp
made her hot, achy. A friend explained the
afternoon play-date was cancelled due to
our girl being black. The friend spoke as though
it was obvious why her mother held
this rule. After the conversation, they
did not know each other. "Friend" must have meant
someone secretly despised, innately
amiss. Without the nuance of deceit
to complicate the error, our dear girl
did wish her friend dead. Not completely dead
by death but silent and still and vanished.
How terrible to hate one's friend, one friend's
mother. One daughter's friend, one's own daughter.

NEW MATH

Some system explained affection between
classmates. When people counted, our girl felt
abstract and outside the sum. Not able
to calculate whose error brought this loss,
she studied zero for her reflection
then practiced insults to equal her peers.
From the empty set, rage and loneliness
factored as natural constants. Those
quick to anger know how it saturates
like ink, too many skies deep. Eventually
worlds would claim her, but that is another
abstraction. At this point, no one knew what
injury they caused. By Wednesday, answers
predicted no escape without a mark.

RECESS

If parents never said friends come in both
pink *and* brown, kids saw the reasons she did
not fit the look or play the part of who
would mom and dad like best. Back then "color
blind" meant thinking anyone could straighten
out if they tried hard enough to be right.
Early in the fall, she felt unwanted
for games though no rejection was mentioned
outright. *Maybe my face is wrong*, she said
with no voice. By winter, lines were drawn
not how she expected. Another black
girl would not speak to her either. Between
them nothing familiar enough to stop
the throb of guilt or anger, who knows which.

ELEMENTARY

How little she loves those who will not have
her, how lonely she suffers a stouthearted
stance. Her words add up to commonplace rhymes,
likely as the habit of pulling down
signs in the little school where she fools them
with her cool dissonance. Syncopation
teaches an elementary listening skill.
She has two hearts: one jumps on the downbeat,
the other on the back. This is how truth
gets tangled up if a line sounds too tight
in dictation, meaning stripped of color.
Draw her as fiction. She cannot recall
why she shares less of her past than lyric
tells, thumping a threat of the obvious.

CRUSH

Push into them first with skin because she
knows her own arouses some friends to skip her
even when she wants to allow them in.
She thinks it hurts when no one can tell how
much space once stood between unconnected
bodies. If anyone said they would pick
her, she would go with them for instruction
in romance, practice kissing all the parts.
More than appetite to bumble over
recesses and amplitudes, a power
in her belly anticipates response.
Shame provokes her to chase boys and bite them,
hit them hard to leave marks all can see, no
matter how dumb desire makes her feel.

SELF

Exclusion from games inspired our girl
to mug sexy for distinction and clout.
On the playground, she shook her fantasy
breasts to fit in. She wanted a body
big enough for her feelings. If you asked
her when she first got angry, she would say
it took twenty years of practicing mean
before sorrow turned rigid on her. Then
she had to cut trouble to bits like her
ego. From town to the next, she discarded
regrets she hoped would never return. But
nerve quivers, keeps pulse with itself even
once removed. She asked me to tell you this
in case you can't hear her voice in this sound.

COGITO

I remain though the same does not apply
to the place that made me sharp. It flickered
out and vanished in storms. The project
of romancing winter relies on salt's
advantage over ice. Snow shields simple
mysteries from the sun. Pretend to know
me, and you will see why we do wrestle
for heat. If I am foreshadowing or
catastrophe, you are delusion or
shell-casing. Neither one of us explains
conflict action alone. Parallel roads
diverge, confirm sadness. From the shoulder,
I count instances of being passed by.
Invisible means I am here, burning.

COLD

I ran anywhere without asking first.
At the end of a road, I met a door
built to close when I called. Years of doors
then the sky turned low and gray on me, too.
Before I could tell God why I shouldn't
be so lonely, a letter explained my
lack of distinction in cursive: *You are*
not what I think of you, it made plain. I
unraveled the words then hand-drew this map
to rescue me from spacelessness. This was
how I first killed the writer. The next time,
I started the story over. The next
time, I let you believe you heard me say
this before, something like this but bitter.

NOTES

"Founding" is based on accounts of the city's history taken from the following sources:

Master Land Use Plan for the City of Troy, Michigan. City of Troy Planning Commission, 1971.

Oakland County Book of History, by Arthur A. Hagman, NYLP, 1970.

Troy Township Pages from History of Oakland County, Michigan, 1877, 2005.

Troy: A City from the Corners, edited by Lorraine Campbell, Arcadia Publishing, 2004.

"Highway" borrows language from Walt Whitman's "Crossing Brooklyn Ferry."

ACKNOWLEDGMENTS

My gratitude goes to the editors of the following print and online journals, who published early versions of some of these poems: *Los Angeles Review* and *Everyday Genius.* "Origin Myths," "Kin," "Resident," "Fear," and "Driveway" appear in *Untitled,* Belladonna chaplet #145.

The New York Foundation for the Arts and Eugene Lang College of The New School University provided generous support.

Thanks to Dan Machlin, Jennifer Tamayo, Ted Dodson, and the rest of the folks at Futurepoem for making this book happen— and additional thanks to the backers of the 2012 Futurepoem Kickstarter initiative.

For encouragement on and joyful distraction from this work, thanks also goes to Toni S. Walters, Jamie K. Walters, Vince Keenan, Jane Charnas, Lee Sartoph, Robert Charnas, Joan Charnas, Tisa Bryant, Jen Hofer, Ruth Ellen Kocher, Douglas Kearney, Adam Mansbach, Matthew Zapruder, Matthew Shenoda, Major Jackson, Alexandra Chasin, Elizabeth Kendall, Margo Jefferson, Craig Taborn, Derek Bermel, Leslie C. Chang, Tracy K. Smith, Amy Benson, Stacy Parker Le Melle, and Isaac Charnas.

For taking care of me throughout this project and sharing in all the challenges that came with it, I am forever grateful to Dan Charnas.

Love to my family.

This first edition, first printing, includes 26 limited edition copies signed by the author and lettered a-z.

This book was set in Spectrum, which is based on the design by Jan van Krimpen in 1943 for the Spectrum Publishing House. Spectrum was completed and released by the Monotype Corporation in 1955, although the Bible project it was originally commissioned for was never completed. Spectrum is known for its readability; its roots reach directly to Venetian typefaces of the 15th century. Its varied weight curves and angular serifs evoke the calligraphic pen strokes of its forebearers.